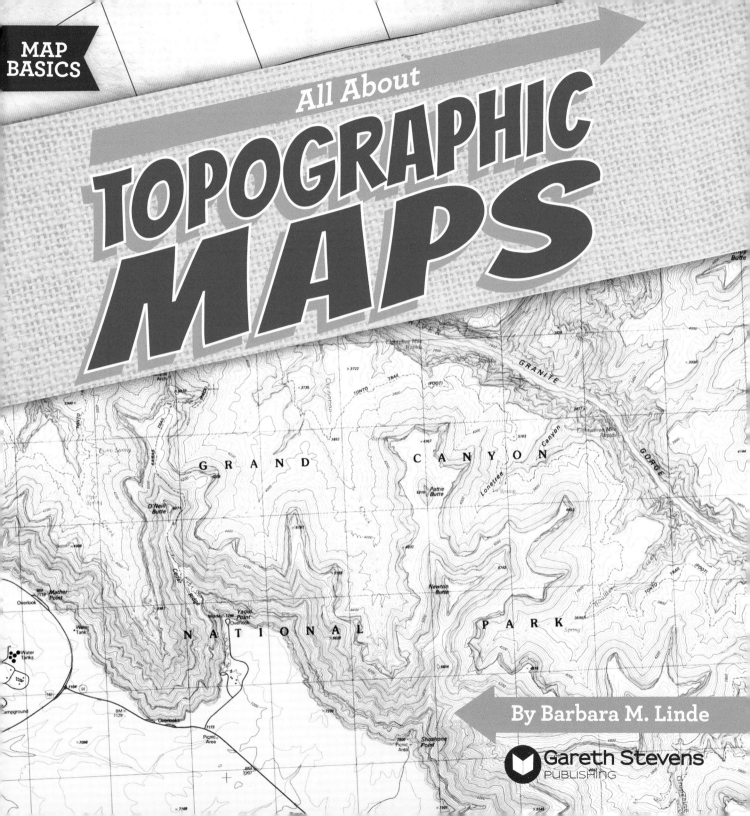

All About

TOPOGRAPHIC MAPS

By Barbara M. Linde

Gareth Stevens
PUBLISHING

Please visit our website, www.garethstevens.com. For a free color catalog of all our high-quality books, call toll free 1-800-542-2595 or fax 1-877-542-2596.

Cataloging-in-Publication Data

Names: Linde, Barbara M.
Title: All about topographic maps / Barbara M. Linde.
Description: New York : Gareth Stevens Publishing, 2019. | Series: Map basics | Includes glossary and index.
Identifiers: ISBN 9781538232705 (pbk.) | ISBN 9781538229200 (library bound) | ISBN 9781538232712 (6pack)
Subjects: LCSH: Topographic maps–Juvenile literature. | Maps–Juvenile literature. | Map reading–Juvenile literature.
Classification: LCC GA130.L56 2019 | DDC 912.01'4–dc23

First Edition

Published in 2019 by
Gareth Stevens Publishing
111 East 14th Street, Suite 349
New York, NY 10003

Designer: Sarah Liddell
Editor: Monika Davies

Photo credits: Cover, pp. 1, 15 U.S. National Park Service, restoration/cleanup by Matt Holly/RKBot/ Wikimedia Commons; p. 5 drlogan/DigitalVision Vectors/Getty Images; pp. 7, 11, 13, 17, 19 courtesy of United States Geological Survey.

Printed in the United States of America

CPSIA compliance information: Batch #CW19GS: For further information contact Gareth Stevens, New York, New York at 1-800-542-2595.

CONTENTS

What Is a Topographic Map? 4

Reading Contour Lines 6

Matching Features and Contour Lines. 8

Important Colors 10

The Legend 12

The Compass Rose 14

Figuring Out Distances. 16

Comparing Topographic Maps 18

Map It!. 20

Glossary. 22

For More Information. 23

Index 24

Words in the glossary appear in **bold** type the first time they are used in the text.

WHAT IS A TOPOGRAPHIC MAP?

Topography is the physical features of an area of land. This includes natural features, such as mountains and lakes. Sometimes man-made features, such as cities and roads, are also included.

Topographic maps show the physical features in an area as if you're looking down on them from above. These maps use wavy lines to show the contour, or outline, and elevation of the land. Elevation is the height of a place above the average height of the sea's surface.

JUST THE FACTS

The Egyptians made one of the first topographic maps around 1150 BC. The Turin **papyrus** map shows the topography of an area in ancient Egypt.

Topographic maps are sometimes called topo maps or contour maps. People use topographic maps for planning outdoor activities, planting crops, building cities, and more.

5

READING CONTOUR LINES

Contour lines show the elevation of the land. All the places along a single contour line are at the same elevation. The number on the line gives the elevation in feet. If you look at a topographic map, you'll notice that contour lines never cross or break.

The **distance** between contour lines is the same on a map, no matter how close together they are. This distance is called the contour interval, and it will be noted somewhere on the map.

JUST THE FACTS
The United States **Geological** Survey (USGS) is a government department that creates and updates topographic maps of the United States.

GOBLIN VALLEY STATE PARK, UTAH

GOBLIN
VALLEY

This topographic map of Goblin Valley State Park in Utah is from the USGS National Map collection. It shows the park's mountains, bodies of water, and flat areas.

MATCHING FEATURES AND CONTOUR LINES

Contour lines that are close together mean elevation is changing quickly and the **slope** is steep. When contour lines are far apart, the slope is gentler because elevation is changing slowly.

The smallest circle within a series of larger circles indicates, or shows, a

mountain peak or hilltop. Sometimes a set of circles will have tick marks. This indicates a depression, or low point, rather than a peak. Contour lines are V or U shaped where they cross rivers and streams. The direction they "point" is upstream.

WHAT YOU SEE ON YOUR MAP

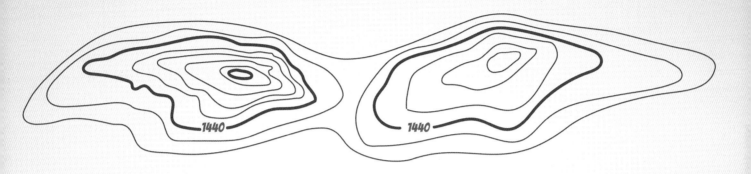

1440   1440

ACTUAL 3D LANDMARK

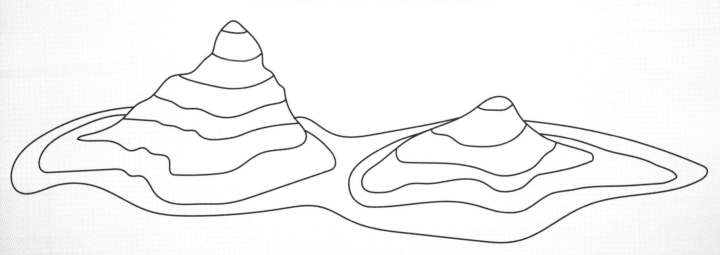

Topographic maps are flat. However, contour lines can help you imagine what the landmarks shown on the map look like in real life.

IMPORTANT COLORS

On a topographic map, contour lines are brown, while bodies of water are blue. Green often shows where thick plant life is growing, and lighter-colored areas show thinner plant life. Areas with lots of buildings are colored red or gray. Main roads are colored red. Other man-made features and smaller roads are black.

This map shows part of Virginia Beach, Virginia. The contour lines are light brown. They're hard to see because there aren't many, which means the land in Virginia Beach is mostly flat.

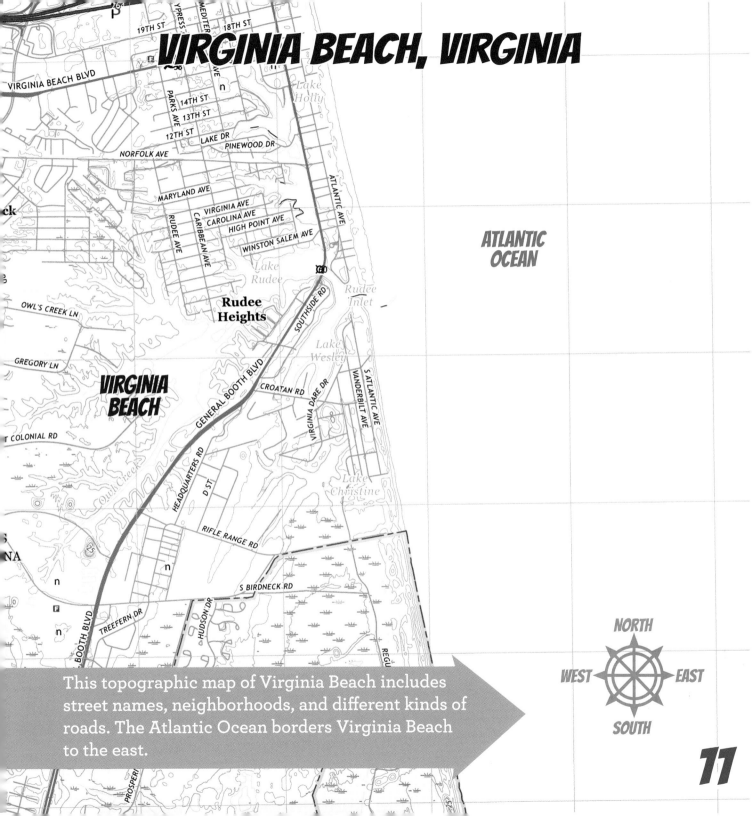

VIRGINIA BEACH, VIRGINIA

ATLANTIC OCEAN

Rudee Heights

VIRGINIA BEACH

This topographic map of Virginia Beach includes street names, neighborhoods, and different kinds of roads. The Atlantic Ocean borders Virginia Beach to the east.

NORTH
WEST EAST
SOUTH

THE LEGEND

Maps use **symbols** to stand for places and things. The legend, or map key, is a list that explains what the symbols mean. The legend may be a box with pictures and text at the bottom of the map. If the legend has a lot of symbols, it might be placed on the back of the map.

JUST THE FACTS

Today, surveyors often use **drones** to create topographic maps. These drones have lasers that can take exact measurements of the land's features.

People often use topographic maps when they visit national parks. A topographic map of a national park may include symbols for campgrounds and areas with picnic tables.

ZION NATIONAL PARK, UTAH

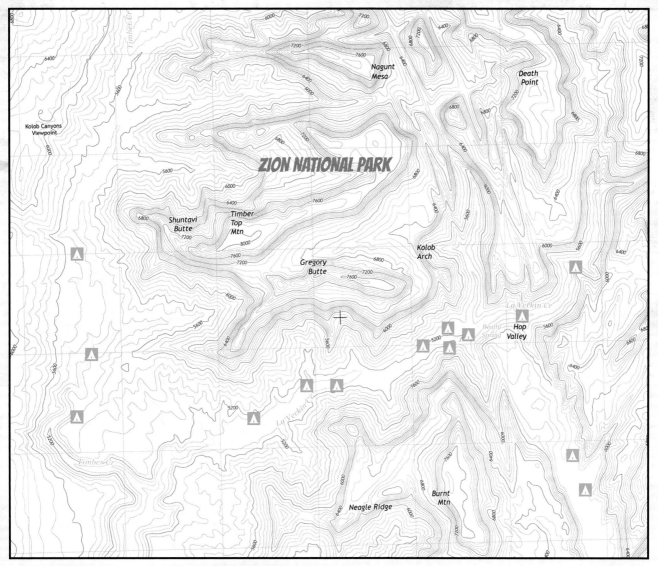

This topographic map of Zion National Park shows where some of the park's campgrounds are located.

THE COMPASS ROSE

Most maps will have a compass rose on them. A compass rose shows the cardinal, or main, directions: north, south, east, and west. North is usually at the top of the map. This means the bottom of the map is south, east is to the right, and west is to the left.

This topographic map shows part of Yellowstone National Park in Wyoming. From Old Faithful you can head southeast to see the Lone Star **Geyser**. Or, you can head east to visit Teal Lake.

JUST THE FACTS

Satellites measure the land from space and send the information to computers on Earth. These measurements help us learn about the topography of places that are hard to get to.

YELLOWSTONE NATIONAL PARK

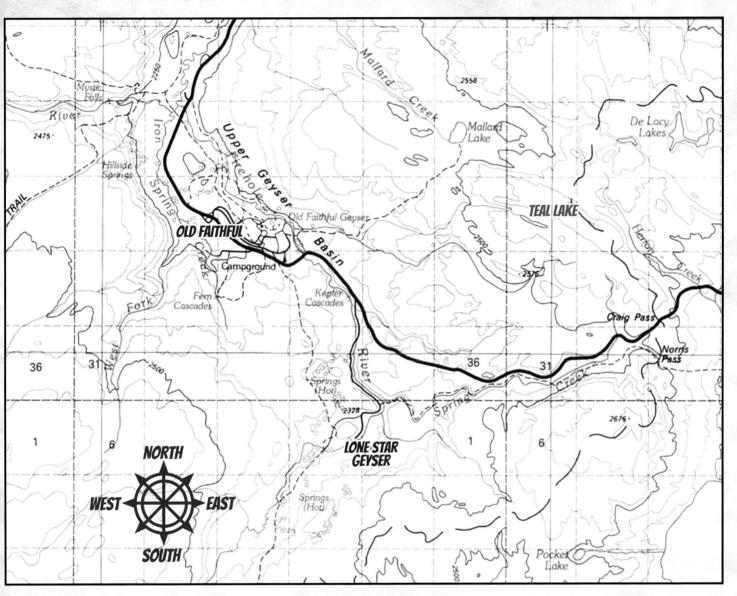

You might find the compass rose at the bottom of the map. Maps have been including a compass rose since the 1300s.

15

FIGURING OUT DISTANCES

Most maps also include a scale. The scale looks like a small ruler and is usually found at the bottom of a map. A map shows a large area of land as smaller than it is in real life. A scale uses a smaller distance to stand for a larger distance.

Interstate 75 (I-75) is a major highway that runs east to west across southern Florida. You can use the scale to figure out how many miles it is from Fort Lauderdale to Naples along I-75.

JUST THE FACTS
Farmers use topographic maps to figure out the best places to plant crops. The military also uses them to understand the shape of the land so they can create battle plans.

SOUTHERN FLORIDA

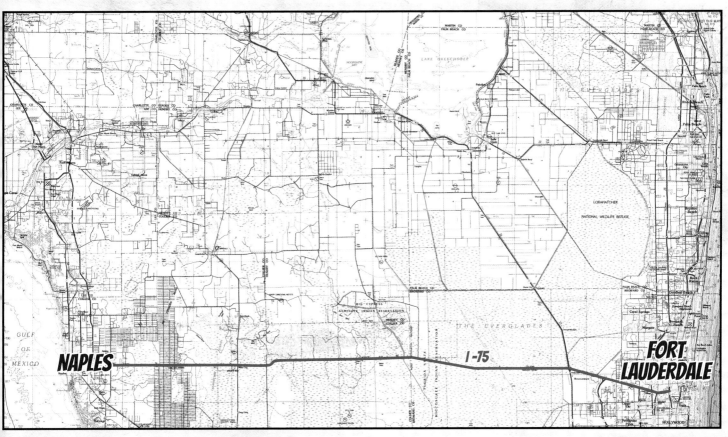

1.5 INCHES

25 MILES

This topographic map of southern Florida shows the area's major highways, roads, bodies of water, and parks. It doesn't have many contour lines because the land of southern Florida is quite flat.

COMPARING TOPOGRAPHIC MAPS

Scientists sometimes compare two or more topographic maps of the same area from different times. This helps them understand how changes caused by both nature and humans have affected an area over time.

Mount Saint Helens is an active volcano in Washington State. Before 1980, the mountain was 9,677 feet (2,950 m) tall, and its top was an evenly shaped cone. On May 18, 1980, the **volcano** erupted. The

JUST THE FACTS
Mount Saint Helens is an active volcano, but people can still climb it! Hikers aren't allowed into the volcano's crater, but they can visit its rim.

explosion blew off the top of the mountain, leaving a large **crater**, with a rim reaching only 8,363 feet (2,549 m) high.

These topographic maps show how the land around Mount Saint Helens looked before and after the eruption in 1980.

MOUNT SAINT HELENS

BEFORE 1980 ERUPTION

AFTER 1980 ERUPTION

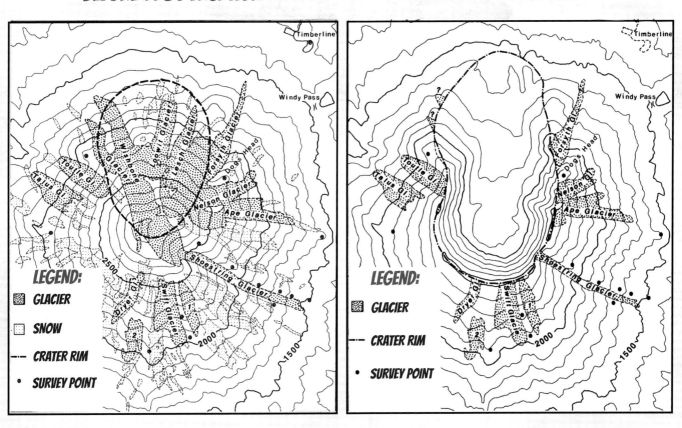

MAP IT!

There are 59 national parks in the United States. This includes well-known parks such as the Everglades National Park in Florida and Glacier Bay National Park in Alaska.

These parks all have fascinating topography. Look at the topography of one of your state's national parks or a park you've always wanted to visit. Look up details about the park's highest and lowest elevations, as well as its natural and man-made features. Once you've looked up the details about the park, share your findings with your classmates!

USE A TOPOGRAPHIC MAP

1 VISIT WWW.NPS.GOV/FINDAPARK/INDEX.HTM OR ASK A LIBRARIAN TO HELP YOU FIND A NATIONAL PARK TO LEARN ABOUT. LOOK UP THE PARK'S TOPOGRAPHIC MAP.

2 CHOOSE A SECTION OF THE MAP AND COPY IT ONTO A LARGE SHEET OF PAPER. USE COLORED MARKERS OR PENCILS TO DRAW THE CONTOUR LINES AS THEY APPEAR ON THE MAP.

3 STUDY THE MAP AND THE LEGEND TO FIND OUT MORE ABOUT THE AREA. DON'T FORGET TO ADD THE SYMBOLS AND A LEGEND TO YOUR COPY OF THE MAP.

4 WRITE A PARAGRAPH THAT WOULD HELP SOMEONE LEARN ABOUT THE AREA. INCLUDE DETAILS ABOUT THE ELEVATION, NATURAL AND MAN-MADE FEATURES, AND AVAILABLE ACTIVITIES IN THE AREA.

GLOSSARY

compass: a tool for finding directions by using a magnetic needle

crater: a bowl-shaped hole on the surface of a planet or moon

distance: the amount of space between two places or things

drone: a type of small aircraft that flies without a pilot

geological: having to do with the rocks, land, and processes of land formation of a certain area

geyser: a spring that shoots heated water and steam from a crack in Earth

papyrus: writing material made from the papyrus plant and used by ancient peoples

satellite: an object that circles Earth in order to collect and send information or aid in communication

slope: ground that slants, or is not level or straight up and down

surveyor: one whose job is to measure land areas

symbol: a picture, shape, or object that stands for something else

volcano: an opening in a planet's surface through which hot, liquid rock sometimes flows

FOR MORE INFORMATION

BOOKS

Maurer, Tracy Nelson. *Using Topographic Maps*. Minneapolis, MN: Lerner Publications, 2017.

Siber, Kate. *National Parks of the USA*. Minneapolis, MN: Wide Eyed Editions, 2018.

Woodward, John. *Geography: A Visual Encyclopedia*. New York, NY: DK Publishing, 2013.

WEBSITES

Make a Topographic Map!
spaceplace.nasa.gov/topomap-clay/en/
Visit NASA's Space Place website and learn how to make your own topographic map.

Reading a Map
www.nps.gov/webrangers/activities/readingmap/
The US National Park Service's interactive introduction to topographic maps will have you reading one in no time!

INDEX

bodies of water 4, 7, 8, 10, 11, 14, 17

cardinal directions 14

compass rose 14, 15

contour intervals 6

contour lines 4, 6, 8, 9, 10, 17, 21

depressions 8

elevation 4, 6, 8, 20, 21

Florida 16, 17, 20

Goblin State Park 7

legend 12, 21

Mount Saint Helens 18, 19

mountains 4, 7, 8, 18

National Map collection 7

national parks 12, 13, 14, 15, 20, 21

peaks 8

roads 4, 10, 11, 17

scale 16

slope 8

surveyors 8, 12

Turin papyrus map 4

United States Geological Survey (USGS) 6, 7, 8, 10

Virginia Beach 10, 11